Bears for Kids

Amazing Animal Books

By Zahra Jazeel

Mendon Cottage Books

JD-Biz Publishing

Read More Amazing Animal Books

Purchase at Amazon.com

Table of Contents

Introduction

Reading can be fun and teach you about lots of things. Today, we are going to learn all about bears.

I am sure you are aware of the teddy bear- the fluffy soft toy with round face and beady eyes almost waiting to be picked and cuddled by someone.

Almost everyone loves the toy for its cuteness. Some may have even wondered if real bears look and feel exactly the same as teddy bears. Wouldn't you love to find out?

Did you know that there are more than 6 different species of bears in the world?

The different sounds of a bear means something specific. Are you curious to know what they mean?

The 'long sleep' or hibernating bears have for certain period of time – what is it called and why do they have such naps?

Want to know more? Then read on as we take you on a journey uncovering all that you need to know about bears starting from habitat, diet, behavior, peculiar habits and different species. All this may sound exciting because this fun filled book will never fail to amaze you with some fascinating facts on bears so much so that you might feel like you are being dragged into a different world with only bears to care for.

About Bears

What comes to your mind when you think of bears? A grizzly bear standing upright baring its teeth ready to shred everything into pieces? Well, if you had that vision, you most probably have heard just one part of the story like many of them. But actually, bears are gentle mammals. They are social and playful too. The closest relative of a bear is the pinniped. There are eight different species of bears in the world living across the Northern and the Southern hemisphere.

Though bears are heavy and big in size, they are well adapted to thrive in land environments as they are very good climbers and fast runners. Their running speeds can reach up to 37mph, though they have a little amount of endurance. Bears are great swimmers too. This ability is beneficial in preying on fish like salmons at certain times of the year.

Mother bears are known to be very protective and affectionate about their cubs and many even fight male adults if they happen to approach her cubs. During autumn, certain bears consume fermented fruits which tend to affect their behavior.

Bears have the ability to identify threatening behavior of humans from non-threatening behavior. Unlike many other animals, they share their resources, security and even friendship. But sadly, these majestic creatures are hunted for food and fur since ancient times.

Features of Bears

Bears have large bodies and they are heavily built. Their fur is shaggy and covers their entire body. They also have a long snout with a short tail. The paws of a bear are said to be plantigrade. That is, when they walk, their whole sole touches the ground. They are very strong and powerful animals with sharp canines and flat molars ideal for their diet.

A bear has a very good sense of hearing and just like the dogs having the ability to hear frequency ranges which humans cannot hear, bears are also sensitive to such high pitches. They also have an excellent sense of smell. The nasal mucosa which plays a major role in sensing smell is present hundred times more in area when compared to a human.

Some animals see pictures in black and white while some others have an infrared vision. But bears have a good color vision like humans. The intelligence of a bear is similar to that of great apes. Each bear is unique individually although they have a clearly established hierarchical order.

Habitats of Bears

Northern hemisphere is home to most bears. But some are found only in North America, Asia, and Europe. However, a bear species known as the Spectacled Bear is native to the South American region of Andes. Hence the Spectacled Bear is also known as the Andean Bear. The only bear once native to Africa was the Atlas Bear which became extinct in the 1870s. It was a subspecies of the Brown Bear. The Brown Bear is the species which is widespread from Western Europe all the way up to the West of North America.

The Polar Bear is limited to the Arctic Sea while the American Bear is found living only in North America. The remaining bear species are found in Asia. Majority of the bears are forest species except the Polar Bear. The Brown Bear may occasionally use tundra or alpine scrub regions to inhabit depending on the yearly season.

Bears usually live in burrows or caves. This is where they sleep for days during the winter. A bear doesn't carve out its territory strictly to defend other bears. In fact, one bear's territory or home range may overlap with another's territory. The size of their territory depends on the availability of food and other needful resources. Hence there can be changes from one year to the next.

Diet of Bears

The diet of many bears contain more plant matter than animal matter. Hence they are omnivores. They are very opportunistic when it comes to food as all bears feed on any food that is available at that time of the year. A research in Taiwan about the Asiatic bears revealed that they consumed a large amount of acorns when it was abundant and switched back to ungulates thereafter.

Smaller bear species which could climb trees have mast as their diet in larger amounts. When they become unavailable, they move on covering a long range of distance looking for other types of food sources. The Polar Bear's diet relies mainly on marine mammals of arctic. The diet of a Giant Panda is mainly on bamboo. The Sloth Bear has a suctioning tongue which is quite long and ideal for feeding on termites, ants and other insects.

Bears are the apex predators in their domain due to their size and power. They prey on carcass and feed on warm blooded animals which are small in size. The only predator to have regularly killed bears which include Sun Bears, small Brown Bears, Sloth Bears, Asiatic Black Bears and Giant Pandas is the tiger.

Behavior and Vocalization

Bears are active most part of the day though some people think they are active only at night, which is not true. This belief may have existed due to the habits of some bears living close to humans. Bears communicate through body language, vocal sounds and scents. Bears are solitary animals. But they can be seen in small groups when female bears are with cubs or when seasonal bounties such as salmons are available. Bears communicate with humans much the same like how they communicate with other bears. Since bears are quite headstrong wanting to have everything in their own way, a slight negotiation is necessary when communicating with them.

A wide variety of vocalization is used by the bears. Moaning is produced as a mild warning if they feel threatened or in fear. Barking is done when they feel excited or alarmed. Huffing is done as a warning signal between the mother and her cubs. Bears growl when they are angry or to give a strong warning. Roaring is similar to growling and used as a sign to intimidate intruders or to proclaim a territory. The cubs make a monotonous, loud buzzing sound which is known as humming.

Much of the body signs of a bear can be identified by a human because it is quite similar to a pet dog.

Asiatic Black Bear

The scientific name of the Asiatic Black Bear directly means the 'Moon bear of the Tibet'. The bear gets this name due to the white crescent shaped patch found on its chest. These bears have long black fur which appear looking thick around the neck and the shoulder region. They stand from four to six feet tall. The bears from the Southern region have a thinner coat than those from the Northern region. The strong claws help them in climbing trees, peeling bark and opening termite mounds.

Asiatic Black Bears mainly live in forests and avoid humans or predators most of the time. Sometimes they sleep on trees. These bears are found in Iran, Afghanistan, Bangladesh, India, China and several other Asian countries. Their diet is made up of honey, fruits, berries, beetle larvae and carrion. Hence they are omnivores. Though some Asiatic Bears tend to hibernate, the others remain active throughout the year depending on the climate and habitat. They feed on nuts during autumn to stay prepared for winter. Most often, these bears are found swimming or splashing in the water in a playful manner.

The IUCN (International Union for Conservation of Nature) has listed the Asian Black Bear as a 'Vulnerable Species' because of habitat loss due to deforestation and selling of bear parts for traditional Chinese medicine.

Black Bear

This is the most abundant bear species in the world. They live in a variety of habitats primarily inhabiting on forest land. They are known to adapt on any region as long as it is a good shelter with food and water. Human encroachment in their area has put them under a serious pressure making them learn how to adjust on new conditions.

North American Black Bears have prominent ears which are quite big. Their sharp claws are curved and aid them in climbing trees. This bear is the fourth largest out of all the eight species of bears in the world. During cold months, most black bears sleep to conserve energy. However the bears living in warmer areas stay active throughout the year.

The diet of a black bear is made up of grass, nuts, insects, fish, rodents, moose, berries and deer fawns. If food becomes unavailable, they resort to finding human-related foods such as pet food, garbage, chickens and homegrown fruit trees.

The lifespan of Black Bears range from 21 to 33 years. They are usually silent and possess an excellent long term memory. Males are bigger in size than the females.

Brown Bear

There are so many varieties of Brown Bears based on their size and color. Hence there are many different yet common names which is why the Brown Bear is called 'The bear with too many names'. The European Brown Bear, Coastal and the Grizzly bear are of the same species except the Kodiak Bear which is a subspecies from the Kodiac Archipelago. Brown Bears inhabit in a variety of habitats and prefer wilderness with less road-density.

The Brown Bear species is the most widespread of all bear species in the world. Though there were more than 50,000 Grizzlies before, sadly there are less than 1200 today living in the wilderness and protected parks within the range of Rocky Mountains in Wyoming, Idaho, Montana and Washington. Brown Bears range from blonde to black in color. But the color may vary with the seasons. They stand 3-4 feet tall on all four feet. Nutrition and gender has an impact on their size.

Brown Bears referred to as Grizzly Bears have a prominent hump on their shoulder. They are omnivores and would defend a carcass ferociously if challenged. Brown Bears rest on dense vegetation during the heat of the day. They are powerful diggers using their claws to dig on rodents, roots or bulbs.

Under the Endangered Species Act, Grizzly Bears are enlisted as a threatened species.

Panda Bear

Due to some unusual features of the Panda Bear, people thought that it was not a bear. However after a debate which lasted for almost a century, the scientists were able to prove that Pandas were in fact a species of bears. They were able to come to this final conclusion by testing the genes of Pandas.

Panda bears are found in China and are disappearing due to human encroachment in their area. They are known to consume stems, leaves and shoots of bamboo varieties. When there is an opportunity, they have meat as well. Among all the other bear species, Pandas are marked distinctly with black and white colorations. The black coloration in their body looks more like red or brown in the wild. They have a small, short tail which is black sometimes. The fur of a Panda is thick with woolly under fur, which is quite dense.

Red Panda Bear

The muscles around their jaw is highly developed which aids them in chewing tough bamboo stalks. The general body structure of Pandas look more like the other bears. They have very flexible forepaws and a unique wrist bone which acts as a 'sixth digit'. They can move around dense forests easily although they lack heel pads on their hind feet.

Pandas usually stay alone trying to avoid each other as best as they could. If they are not found eating, they may as well be resting or lazing around. It is impossible to accumulate fat with a diet of bamboo to sleep during winter. Hence the Pandas move to lower elevations having warm weather and plenty of food. They are active mostly in the early evening and in dawn. The Giant Panda has become a universal symbol of conservation apart from being a national treasure of China.

Polar Bear

Polar bear, also known as 'Sea Bears' are the largest species among all bears. They live in the Arctic Circle and are facing a threat due to the negative impacts of global warming, tourism and various kinds of pollution. The Polar Bear is quite adaptable to deal with extreme temperatures though they are not found living in Antarctic region.

60% of the wild Polar Bear population of the world lives in Canada. The fur of a Polar bear appears to be pure white or yellow depending n the light. Their black skin helps in absorbing the heat of the sun.

Polar Bears are among the largest land predators and can reach up to 4 feet or more at shoulder level. The muscles in their neck and hind legs are well developed and the paws are webbed to aid in swimming. Certain areas in their feet are not covered in fur and appear rough to prevent them slipping on ice.

The diet of a Polar Bear is mainly on seals and other marine mammals or birds. They are excellent predators and most often consume only the skin and fat of their prey leaving the rest for scavengers. This is because a lot of energy and water is necessary to digest meat. Polar Bears spend more time in water hunting for food or escaping from danger.

The Inuit people who lived thousands of years ago are said to have coexisted with Polar Bears occasionally killing them for food or clothing. But they never overhunted these creatures.

Sloth Bear

Sloth bears have a unique appearance and a docile nature. They are most often confused with sloth, another tropical animal. These bears inhabit the warm and humid forests of South East Asia, preferably close to the equator. There are 2 known subspecies. They are the Indian Sloth Bear and the Sri Lankan Sloth Bear. There are also reported sightings in Nepal, Bangladesh and Burma.

The fur of a Sloth bear is long, black and shaggy particularly around their necks appearing like a mane. In contrast, the insides of their legs and belly area have little fur. There is a white patch of hair in the shape of U or Y on their chests. They stand up to 3 feet tall at shoulder level. They possess no front teeth and have a long tongue and protruding lips perfectly designed to suck termites from mounds. Sometimes the sucking sounds could be heard from far away.

These bears are active at night and sleep during the day. They prefer to be alone and are excellent climbers of trees. Although they prefer termites to have mostly, they also consume plants and animal matter as well. These bears do not have the need for hibernation due to the availability of termites and ants as required.

Spectacled Bear

Spectacled Bear is also known as the Andean Bear because they are found only in the Andes mountainous region in South America. The eyes of these bears have light colored rings around them making it appear like they're wearing spectacles and that is how they get their name as 'Spectacled Bears'. Not much is known about these bears due to the lack of research. However, they are known to be shy and avoid human contact as much as possible.

They have shaggy fur which range in colors from black to brown. But their fur is thinner compared to the North American Bear species since they are found to live in warm climates. When it comes to size, females are little smaller than the males. Spectacled Bears can climb on trees very well due to their long claws.

Though these bears are omnivores occasionally having meat apart from plant matter, they love fruit trees and could be seen eating and sleeping for days in fruit trees. They do not have to hibernate since they live in warm climate with food in abundance all year. The fascinating thing about these bears is that they are the only members surviving from the subfamily of Tremarctinae. Interestingly, these types of bears held a very special place in the religious beliefs of ancient Incans.

Sun Bear

Sun Bear is the smallest among all the other species of bears. Researching on this type of bears is a hard task since they are rare to find. They live in hot and humid regions living on trees foraging for various types of fruits and insects as a major source of protein in their diet. Deforestation is a serious threat to their habitat.

Sun Bears possess black fur which is dense and sleek. Their thick coat helps in protecting them from mud, insects and dirt. A distinctive feature of Sun Bears is their long tongue and snout designed to extract honey and bee larvae. They sleep during the day and forage for food at night time. Since they live in a warm climate with plenty of food, hibernation is not necessary. In fact, they remain active throughout the year.

Sun Bears have the largest canines of all other bear species in relation to size. Their paws are strong with claws in the shape of sickles. The fur of a female bear is slightly longer than a male. In order to scare away unwelcome guests or predators, these bears bark as a warning.

The IUCN (International Union for Conservation of Nature) enlisted Sun Bears as a vulnerable species in 2007. Though laws were written in order to protect these bears, implementation is lacking.

Bears and Humans

It must be surprising to hear but bears are shy creatures and avoid humans most of the time. They become easily frightened but when provoked, they can attack and injure a person seriously. Since all bears are physically powerful, it is best not to test them because they are capable to do some serious damage not only to humans but other resources and properties too.

Bear species such as the Brown Bear, Polar Bear, American Black Bear and Sloth Bear can be dangerous to humans in places where they are used to being around people. Bear attacks on humans are reported widely though such incidents occur rarely. The dangers posed by bears towards humans are exaggerated through human imagination. However it should be noted that if the cubs feel threatened, mother bears behave ferociously defending and attacking the unwelcome guests. This could bring about tragic results to the unfortunate intruders.

Some instances where bears come into conflict with humans is when they attack livestock or raid crops. In order to protect the bears from habitat loss, many laws have been passed in certain regions of the world. Bear's intelligence have been put to use by people even centuries before by training them to perform in circuses and do tricks like bicycle riding, dancing etc. During the late 20th century, using bears for these purposes became controversial.

Myths and Legends

Bear is an animal used in several cultures from ancient times due to its magnificent physique and strength. Most tribes attributed to fishing and hunting worshipped bear as a sacred animal while most

Siberian people and prehistoric Finns considered bear to be the spirit of their forefathers. Hence bears were respected and valued. The national animal of Finland is also the bear.

The traditional fairy tale of Russia speaks of a boy named Ivan who attempts to kill a mother bear along with her cubs and was punished by having his head turned into a bear's head and finally shunned by the entire community.

Koreans identify bears as symbolic animals and consider them to be their ancestors. One Korean legend states that a God made a she-bear to pass a difficult test and when she completed it successfully, the bear was turned into a woman and the God married her eventually.

Bears are worshipped in early China and in Ainu cultures. In the Alpine zone, legends about saints taming bears are common. Bears are popular in today's children's stories like 'Winnie the Pooh' and 'Goldilocks and the three Bear'. There are even animated movies like 'The Brother Bear' and 'Care Bears' featuring bears as lead roles.

Author Bio

Fathima Zahra Jazeel

Was born in Sri Lanka and completed her G.C.E Advanced Level in the Bio Science stream. She completed her BTEC Level IV Edexcel Professional Diploma in Teaching in the year 2013 and currently works as a teacher while following the BTEC Level V Edexcel Professional Diploma in Advanced Teaching leading to a professional degree. Her passion for journalism made her engage in writing for both local, as well as international news magazines.

Her family had been rearing parrots as pets for decades which motivated her to be a local voluntary social worker to create awareness about conserving animals in the wild.

Our books are available at

1. Amazon.com

2. Barnes and Noble

3. Itunes

4. Kobo

5. Smashwords

6. Google Play Books

Download Free Books!

http://MendonCottageBooks.com

Publisher

JD-Biz Corp

P O Box 374

Mendon, Utah 84325

http://www.jd-biz.com/

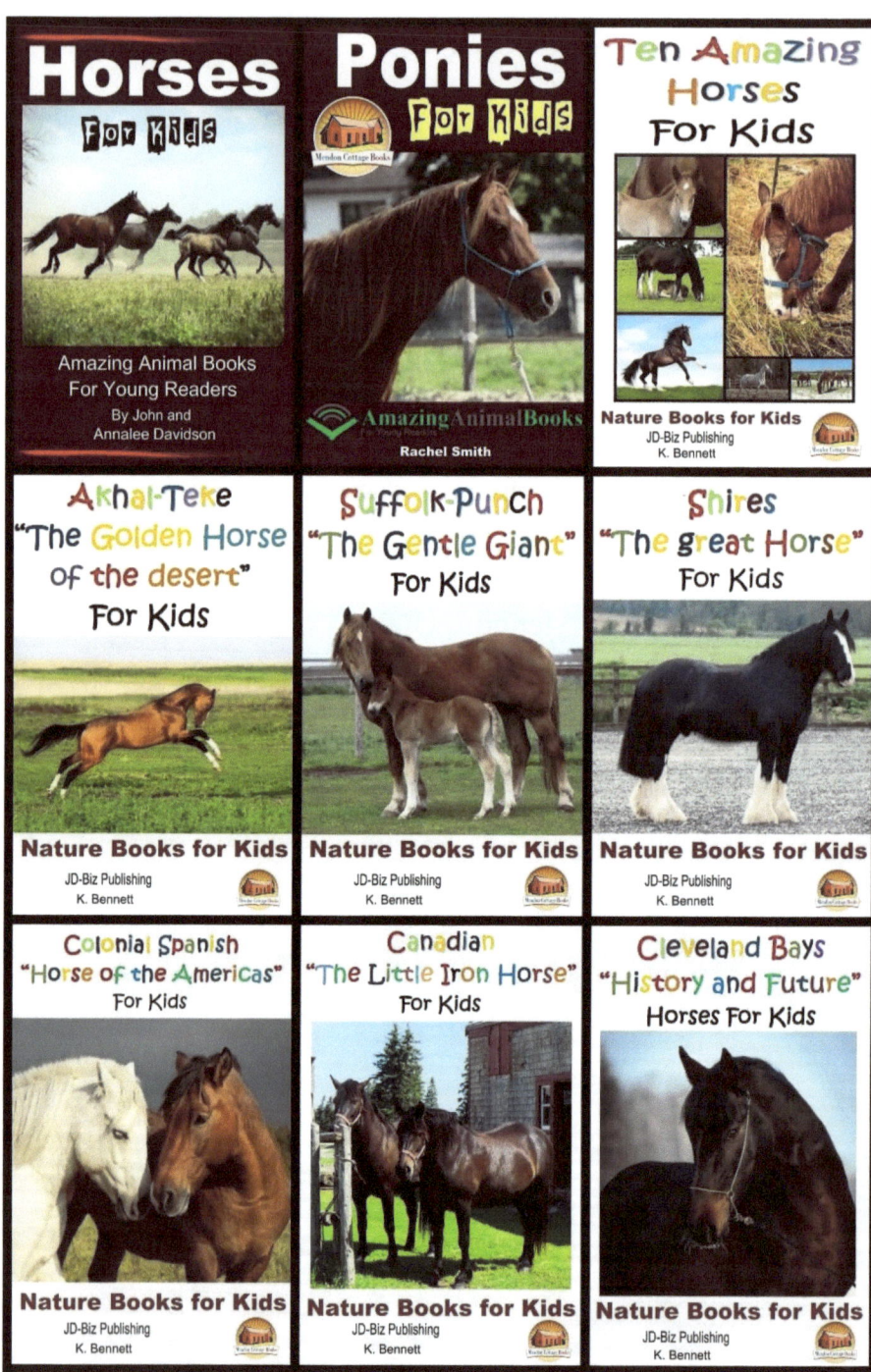

Horses For Kids

Amazing Animal Books
For Young Readers
By John and
Annalee Davidson

Ponies For Kids

Meridian Cottage Books

Amazing Animal Books
For Young Readers
Rachel Smith

Ten Amazing Horses For Kids

Nature Books for Kids
JD-Biz Publishing
K. Bennett

Akhal-Teke "The Golden Horse of the desert" For Kids

Nature Books for Kids
JD-Biz Publishing
K. Bennett

Suffolk-Punch "The Gentle Giant" For Kids

Nature Books for Kids
JD-Biz Publishing
K. Bennett

Shires "The great Horse" For Kids

Nature Books for Kids
JD-Biz Publishing
K. Bennett

Colonial Spanish "Horse of the Americas" For Kids

Nature Books for Kids
JD-Biz Publishing
K. Bennett

Canadian "The Little Iron Horse" For Kids

Nature Books for Kids
JD-Biz Publishing
K. Bennett

Cleveland Bays "History and Future" Horses For Kids

Nature Books for Kids
JD-Biz Publishing
K. Bennett

Bears

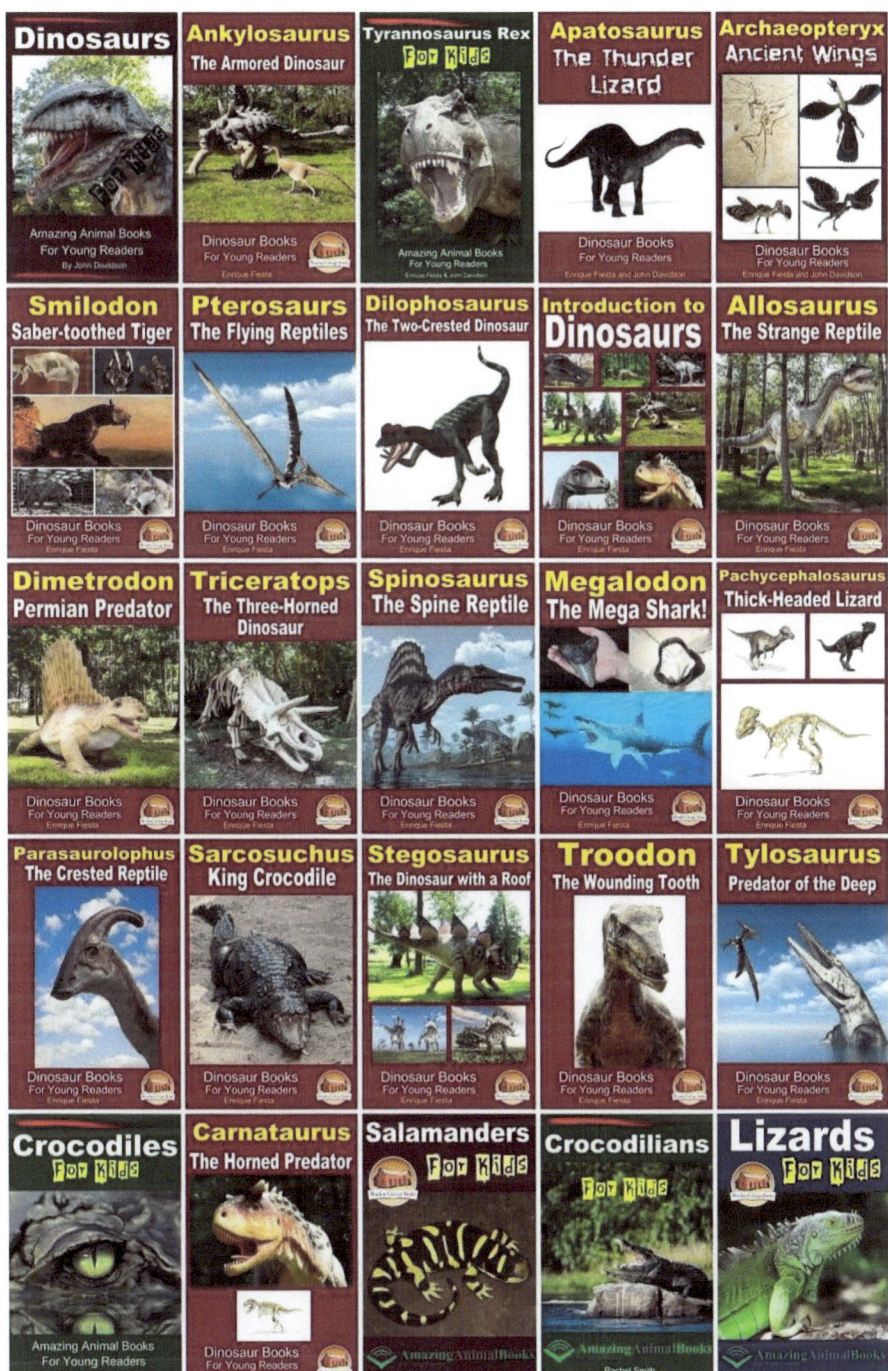

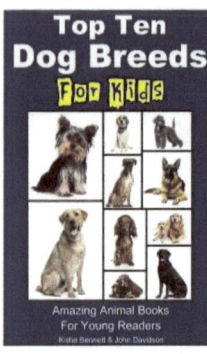

Top Ten Dog Breeds For Kids

Amazing Animal Books For Young Readers
Kisha Bennett & John Davidson

German Shepherds

Dog Books for Kids
K. Bennett

Bulldogs

Dog Books for Kids
K. Bennett

Dachshund

Dog Books for Kids
K. Bennett

Poodles

Dog Books for Kids
K. Bennett

Labrador Retrievers

Dog Books for Kids
K. Bennett

Rottweilers

Dog Books for Kids
K. Bennett

Boxers

Dog Books for Kids
K. Bennett

Golden Retrievers

Dog Books for Kids
K. Bennett

Puppies

Dog Books For Kids

Amazing Animal Books
By John Davidson

Beagles

Dog Books for Kids
K. Bennett

Yorkshire Terriers

Dog Books for Kids
K. Bennett

Dogs
Top Ten Dog Breeds For Kids

Amazing Animal Books For Young Readers
Zahra Jazeel & John Davidson

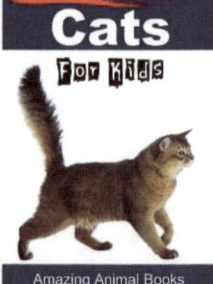

Cats For Kids

Amazing Animal Books For Young Readers
K. Bennett & John Davidson

Foxes For Kids

Amazing Animal Books For Young Readers
Zahra Jazeel & John Davidson

Wolves For Kids

Amazing Animal Books For Young Readers
By John Davidson and Virginia Fidler